Even Good Girls Get Mad at God

Heal Your Anger And Learn To Trust God Again

HOPE WILBANKS

This book has been written to provide information. It is sold with the understanding that the author and publisher are not engaged in rendering professional medical advice. Please seek the services of a competent professional, if required. This book should be used as a guide – not as the ultimate source of information about this topic.

The author and publisher does not warrant that the information contained in this book is fully complete and shall not be responsible for any errors or omissions. The author and publisher shall have neither liability nor responsibility to any person or entity with respect to any loss or damage caused or alleged to be caused directly or indirectly by this book.

Scripture quotations marked (NLT) are taken from the Holy Bible, New Living Translation, copyright © 1996, 2004, 2007 by Tyndale House Foundation. Used by permission of Tyndale House Publishers, Inc., Carol Stream, Illinois 60188. All rights reserved.

Scripture quotations marked (AMP) are taken from the Amplified® Bible, Copyright © 1954, 1958, 1962, 1964, 1965, 1987 by The Lockman Foundation. Used by permission. (www.Lockman.org)

Copyright © 2011 Hope Wilbanks
evengoodgirlsgetmadatgod.com

All rights reserved.

DEDICATION

This book is dedicated to Robert, who bore my cross of anger alongside me, and loved me through the pain to healing. I love you forever.

And for you, hurting and hiding your anger. Jesus loves you.

CONTENTS

	Acknowledgments	i
1	Introduction	1
2	The Root of Anger	Pg 6
3	Lies That Fuel Your Anger	Pg 8
4	What Anger Does to Your Body and Mind	Pg 11
5	Anger Hurts Your Loved Ones	Pg 14
6	Anger Destroys Your Faith	Pg 16
7	Anger Thrives on Doubt and Confusion	Pg 20
8	Anger Causes You to Withdraw	Pg 22
9	Get Real With God	Pg 25
10	Tell Him Why You're Angry	Pg 27
11	Jesus Showed Anger Towards His Disciples	Pg 29
12	Jesus Showed Anger Towards People	Pg 31
13	Jesus Was Angry at God, His Father	Pg 33
14	Healing Restoration	Pg 35
15	Reconcile With God	Pg 37
16	Guard Your Soul and Mind	Pg 40

ACKNOWLEDGMENTS

There is One friend who has been with me through all the ups and downs in life. Without Him I know I would not be who I am or where I am today: His name is Jesus. He loves without end, forgives every sin, and makes messy hearts clean and whole. I could never have written this book without His guidance or blessing. I love You, Jesus!

Millions of thanks to my best friend, Angela Klocke. You've also stood by me through dark hours and lonely days. We've laughed together and shared many tears. I have no doubt God ordained this friendship. I love you...more.

Thanks to my two little sisters, Crystal and Faith. You listen to me whine and encourage me when I need it most. Thank you both for being my biggest cheerleaders. I love you both.

INTRODUCTION: MY STORY

Salty tears streaked my cheeks. For the umpteenth time I cried again. Pain pierced my heart. Frustration roared through my veins.

I was mad at God.

In the previous year, I'd been Momma and Daddy to my children while my husband was on his second tour of duty in Iraq. It was a tough year, full of worry, stress, and tension.

Somehow the kids and I managed to settle into a routine, though. We relocated to a new community, school, and church in Tennessee. My kids were happy. For the first time in a very long time, I was content as well, despite the circumstances.

When my husband's deployment ended, he came home and went back to work in Louisiana. The kids and I stayed nearly five hundred miles away, so they could finish out their school year. When it had come to an end, we packed up and moved back to Louisiana to be with my husband.

I went kicking and screaming.

I didn't want to leave Tennessee. I'd found contentment through serving God at our new church. I'd stepped into the role of Sunday School teacher in a classroom of pre-teen girls. I knew God was using me to make a difference. So why would He force me to leave that place of peace and security, and send me back to where I didn't want to be?

It didn't make sense to me.

After the move, I mourned for months. I begged God to make a way for us to be where I wanted to be. I pleaded with Him, "I felt so loved and accepted there, God! Don't You want me to be happy?!"

The hurt cut my heart and soul deep.

As the questions in my mind increased, so did the anger in my heart. If God was such a loving, kind Father, why would He do this to me? I couldn't grasp it. I didn't want to understand it. I was furious with God.

My husband became frustrated with me. The madder I became at God, the wider the fracture between my husband and I expanded. I was angry at him, too. He was the one, after all, who decided we needed to go back to Louisiana. He was the one who didn't seem willing to relocate to Tennessee.

It was all his fault.

And God's.

This turmoil continued for months. Depression's dark cloud settled in over my mind and spirit. I didn't even realize it, because I was so busy being mad at God.

I distinctly recall one Saturday when I succumbed to my grief and depressive thoughts. I couldn't make myself get out of bed. I blankly stared at the wall. There were no words.

I wanted to curl up and die. If this was the life God meant for me, I didn't want any part of it.

Bitterness snowballed to massive proportions. I was angry at God. Angry at my husband. Irritated at my children.

I just wanted to die.

Have you ever been there? Done with life? Done with God?

This single incident brought intense feelings and emotions to the surface. But the anger in my heart didn't occur instantly and only because of this situation. The hurt started long before and clung to my heart for many years.

The ugly truth is I've experienced a lot of pain in my life. It's taken me the better part of my life to work through that pain.

Sometimes I still struggle with the pain from my past.

Very few people know about my distressful childhood. Even fewer understand the depth of pain I endured and still deal with today.

I have limited memories up to about the age of nine or ten. The majority of those memories are not good.

Verbal abuse.

Emotional abuse.

Sexual abuse.

Emotional abandonment.

I sincerely believe if it weren't for God's hand on my life, I would've never made it through those experiences with a sane mind.

During my teen years, I struggled with this mistreatment, with exception of the sexual abuse. By then, the trauma of the other forms of abuse weighed so heavy on me that I couldn't focus or think at times during school. The anguish was nearly more than I could bear.

When I was in seventh grade, I became so distraught that I wrote a letter to a friend, explaining that I couldn't bear the suffering any longer and wanted to die. I told her I was going to take every pill I could find in the medicine cabinet after school that day.

Thankfully, she did what any good friend would do; she turned the note into the assistant principal. Unfortunately, my cries for help went unheard and that counseling session was unproductive on many levels.

Through this period of time, I learned how to protect myself in a way that many victims of abuse learn: I turned everything inward. I shut off my real feelings from the world. Never tried to reach out for help again.

Because nobody would believe the horrible things I witnessed and experienced at home.

After graduating high school, I left home. My self-esteem gradually blossomed. But even though I became more confident in myself, I still had a long way to go.

My husband and I married in 1997. Little did I know this would be the beginning of a long healing process for me, and my husband would become the interim "doctor" to help aid in my recovery.

God is ever-faithful in supplying our needs.

Over the last fourteen years, my husband and I have lived through quite a bit together. At times we've lovingly held hands, while other times we've walked in silence until God pulled us back together again.

I know what it's like to…
- have overdue bills you can't pay.
- lose a baby due to a miscarriage.

- be without transportation (while pregnant and with a toddler in tow).
- feel out of place at church.
- be so depressed you want to die.
- watch your marriage crumble apart (then witness God putting it back together).
- find peace after the storms.

Anger doesn't pop up overnight. It's a culmination of things happening over a period of time. Things that you think you've moved beyond, but then they suddenly creep up again the next time something bad happens.

I was angry at God for making me move, but that anger was a result of me harboring years of frustration over not understanding why certain things happened.

Sister, as you read this book, my prayer is that God will use my experiences to open your eyes to understanding. I pray you'll feel God's loving embrace, find the answers you need, and discover the peace that passes all understanding.

I have a feeling some of you reading this book may be doing so out of curiosity. You're interested in hearing about how someone could possibly be angry at God. You're especially interested in knowing why God didn't strike me dead for being angry at Him.

Or maybe you've been taught that you aren't supposed to be mad at God. Or that God's an angry God. And so if you are angry, you think you have to hide it because terrible things might happen if you speak the truth.

Please allow me to dispel these thoughts.

Before you begin, let me fill you in on a little secret: It's okay to be mad at God. Even good girls get mad at God.

THE ROOT OF ANGER

Anger roots weed-like in your heart. When the seed is planted, it grows wild. It digs down deep and forges a life of its own.

The Bible refers to bitterness as a poisonous root in Hebrews 12:15 (NLT), "...Watch out that no poisonous root of bitterness grows up to trouble you, corrupting many." Anger manifests itself through bitterness.

Bitterness corrupts. It damages and destroys your integrity—with man and God. It alters who you are and how you think.

Inexplicable situations in life, like a loss or financial strain, fertilize those seeds of bitterness. Before long, and maybe without you even realizing it, thorny vines of resentment choke your spirit. Then the questions begin.

Why me?

Isn't this the question we've all asked God? Something bad happens. You don't understand it. You can't see the good in it. So you start asking God, "Why?"

Because you find your particular situation difficult to understand, you also question God's intentions. If God has a purpose for your life, surely His plan does not include so many incomprehensible things happening to you. Right?

"And by the way, God," you might continue, "How could You leave me, when I've done so much for you?"

Now, isn't that so typical of our flesh?

Meanwhile, the devil snickers. You're right where he wants you. Bitter. And if you aren't careful, you'll start listening to the lies he whispers in your ear.

God doesn't love you. God doesn't care about you. God isn't anywhere near you.

Lies.

Peter said, "Stay alert! Watch out for your great enemy, the devil. He prowls around like a roaring lion, looking for someone to devour" (1 Peter 5:8, NLT). The devil waits for these opportunities to sneak in and snatch you away from God.

LIES THAT FUEL YOUR ANGER

As bitterness grows, disappointment hardens your heart. With every passing day, you question God more and more.

There are three common lies we tell ourselves in the midst of such confusion and doubt:

1. I pray, but God isn't listening to me.
2. I've been faithful to God, but now He's left me when I need Him the most.
3. If God doesn't have control of this, then I might as well do whatever I want and forget about Him.

Let's take a look at each of these lies.

God isn't listening to me when I pray. So why should I keep trying to live right? Why should I keep praying? It's pointless.

God hears every prayer, but we expect Him to answer us the way we think He should. We don't pray for His answer; we pray for Him to provide us with the answer we've already devised to be the perfect solution.

If only it worked that way.

Maybe you've thought lately, I've been faithful to God all these years and now, when I need Him the most, He's nowhere to be found.

It simply isn't true. He promises in Hebrews 13:5 (NLT), "...I will never fail you. I will never abandon you." That's a standing promise. Period.

Perhaps the most damaging lie is that God isn't in control. That He has abandoned you and because you can't see Him anymore, your life is in utter chaos.

I might as well do whatever I want and forget about seeking His face. It's pointless. He's gone.

Sister, if you're having any of these thoughts, hear me when I tell you they are not truth. They are lies from the father of all lies—satan. He would love nothing more than for you to believe you're alone and that God has forgotten or abandoned you. But it isn't true.

No matter how mad you are at God, He's still there. If you believe those lies long enough though, they'll become your truth. Then disobedience will creep through the back door of your heart.

Do you sometimes question everything you've ever believed about God? Does doubt breed deeper confusion and uncertainty in your mind? Are you making choices based on that doubt? Do you feel like you're plummeting into a bottomless pit and things keep getting worse rather than better?

I understand that helpless—hopeless—feeling. I've been where you are. Many times.

WHAT ANGER DOES TO YOUR BODY & MIND

Do you feel exhausted all the time? Tired for no reason? Stressed out? Fearful?

Have you cried uncontrollably lately? Felt like a failure? Wanted to die?

Anger is a vicious monster. It rots your soul from the inside-out.

After the birth of my son in 2003, I suffered from post-partum depression. I didn't know what was wrong with me. I just knew something wasn't right.

"I have no desire to hold my baby," I cried to my doctor. "What's wrong with me?"

Consequently, I began taking medication, which tremendously helped me get out of that pit.

The post-partum depression I experienced was a physical depression.

It had absolutely nothing to do with my spirituality. It was simply, purely a physical problem.

However, I do believe physical depression certainly can lead to spiritual depression, if it isn't attended to and taken control of with authority. This is precisely what happened to me during those months of being mad at God for not giving me my way.

A spiritual depression sinks into your soul and renders your body and mind incapacitated. It's healed only by God. No man-made medication can take away a spiritual depression.

Did you ever play the game "Trust" as a child? You'd stand in front of someone and fall backwards into their (presumably) waiting arms. But how often did you actually trust the person standing behind you enough to release yourself?

I can't help but compare this simple game to my real-life trust issues with God.

When something (bad) happened, I'd stiffen. Instead of falling back into the arms of God, I'd catch myself just short of falling into His arms.

Shoulders hunched. Worry lines creviced my forehead. And I'd walk away. Unwilling. Untrusting.

Been there?

It isn't a tiny incident that leads to this mistrust. It's problem after problem. It's feeling like you haven't recovered from the last battle, before you're bombarded with yet another round of bullets. You can't wrap your mind around it. You start feeling like you're all alone.

Like maybe God isn't there anymore.

Your mind is a powerful weapon. The devil knows this and he will use every tactic in his back pocket to attack your mind.

When you slam the door of your heart in anger to God, you open the window of your mind to the devil.

ANGER HURTS YOUR LOVED ONES

"You don't understand what I'm going through!" I yelled at my husband. "I don't want to be here. I miss my church family!"

As soon as I shouted the angry words I wanted to take them back, but I couldn't.

Face flushed, he gritted his teeth. "I do understand, Hope, but you're mad at me for something I can't help!" He walked outside, slamming the door behind him.

In the process of ignoring God, I'd started turning my angry thoughts towards my family. My sweet husband bore the brunt of this. (I stand amazed at how patient he was with me.)

I wouldn't voice my anger to God. I didn't want to talk to Him. Instead, I lashed out at those I loved.

All that pent-up anger boiled in my heart and foamed over onto my husband and children. It was like watching myself turn into a person I didn't recognize. I didn't like it, but I didn't know how to stop it either.

Anger is like that. It wraps tight around your heart and chokes out life.

You might think you're doing a great job of masking your anger, but your family knows something isn't right. Your friends note the change in your attitude and spirit. And despite your attempt to hide your feelings, the ones you love are often the ones who are affected the most.

ANGER DESTROYS YOUR FAITH

When we moved back to Louisiana, I was miserable. I tried to hide it. I prayed for change. I begged for months. "Lord, please move us back north. Please make a way. Please provide a job. Please…"

Nothing.

No answer.

I felt like God turned a deaf ear.

Ever felt like that? Alone? Empty? Angry?

There was another thought process I struggled with during this time. Having grown up in church, I was what many would call a "good girl." I didn't participate in many of the worldly things so many desired. Yet there I was—the good girl—angry at God.

"Good girls" aren't supposed to get mad at God…right?

This is yet another ploy of the devil. It's an obvious tactic. He would love nothing more than to make you believe your anger is a horrible sin, especially since you're supposed to be a light to the world.

Some shining example you are. What kind of faith is that? Maybe you don't have any faith at all. If your faith's so great, wouldn't God run to your rescue this very moment and give you exactly what you're asking for?

Truth is you're human and humans aren't perfect. You get mad. You have questions. Your emotions overwhelm you sometimes. That doesn't make you any less worthy of grace.

It doesn't mean your faith isn't enough.

It doesn't mean God doesn't hear.

Singer and songwriter Alle McCloskey of The Alleluia Journey shares her faith-shaken testimony:

> *I felt His whisper and I had answered, "Here am I, send me." I had attended every meeting, started packing my bags, raised all the funds I needed and then some, prepped with my team for the programs we would be presenting; it was all coming together. This was to be my first trip to our church plant in inner city D.C. and I was pumped!*
>
> *I kept imagining the friendships I would find. The children who would enter the Kingdom of God through the messages in our VBS programs. The "out of my comfort zone" experiences I would be able to bring home to share with family and friends. I was so excited to see what God was going to do in and through me. It felt like a new chapter of my life.*

Then, slowly, things began to shift. In my heart, I sensed God quietly whispering "not this time." But I ignored it, telling myself that He had provided in every way for me to go on this trip. Why would He snatch this opportunity from me at the last minute?

It wasn't fair. Besides, wasn't I going to do His work, to share His story and love? How could He say no now?

I plunged ahead, but life began to change. Episodic dizziness set in and then migraines. I told myself it was stress and would clear up, but it didn't. It escalated to the point that I was forced to forgo the trip. I had to watch my friends leave, and then hear their incredible stories of what God did in D.C. after the fact.

I was angry with God taking the trip away from me and I was even more angry with Him for my newly-acquired health issue.

I doubted His love and goodness.

I had been so willing to be obedient to His call to take His message to people who didn't know His love. I was ready to do whatever He asked. Well, everything except stay home.

I poured those emotions into a new song. Words and melodies flowed together in a desperate challenge to Him. I connected with David's cries in the Psalms, where he voices his fears of God's abandonment in the midst of enemies. It was one of the rawest pieces I'd ever written.

God has allowed me to use the transparency I found during those darker days to reach others. Through that song, I've seen God's presence and love spill into the hearts of people who were afraid to admit that they've felt like a stranger to their Maker, or that they're struggling with simply believing.

It's been years since that missed mission's trip. I've moved past the anger and uncertainty of God's perfect will because I've seen how He redeems all things to His glory.

He is big enough to handle that doubt. He is strong enough to carry us when we're kicking and screaming like an angry child. He is God enough to take that which we don't understand and use it for His divine purposes.

ANGER THRIVES ON DOUBT & CONFUSION

When I became pregnant with our second child in 2001, we were ecstatic. Then everything fell apart.

Near the end of my first trimester, my two-year old daughter and I were in a vehicle accident. Less than a week later, I miscarried our baby.

My husband and I were devastated.

During the week this happened, he took personal time from work to be home. He wanted to care for me and grieve our loss together. When he returned to work the following week, he was given a pink slip. He was fired for taking off the week to be with me during our loss.

Confusion? An understatement.

Doubt? You bet.

It's really difficult to understand the why in such circumstances.

Anger makes you feel like your life is spinning out of control.

You doubt God cares.

You're confused about what's happening. You can't understand it and you don't see God's purpose. You aren't even sure if there is a purpose anymore.

Bad stuff keeps happening. No matter how hard you try, there's nothing you can do to stop or change these things.

Confusion fogs your mind. You're so angry that you don't even want to bring your concerns and thoughts to the Lord in prayer.

If you're stuck in that awful crevice, I want to remind you of something that will hopefully help you out: You can't stop bad things from happening. You don't have the power to prevent some things from taking place. You aren't in control of life.

God is.

I know it's overwhelming. I understand what it's like to doubt or believe that He cares.

In the middle of your chaos, there is one fact you can take to the bank. He is there. He sees your heartache. He knows the pain. He understands your questions.

ANGER CAUSES YOU TO WITHDRAW

At the peak of my anger towards God, I withdrew from everyone and everything. My anger turned into depression. I didn't care about anything anymore. I was empty. Hopeless.

If God wasn't going to answer my prayers for help—if He wouldn't give me what I wanted—there was no point in living.

Reflecting on it now, I can see how childish and foolish I acted. But at that time, I was angry and couldn't understand why God forced me in a direction I didn't want to go.

So I retreated. I attended church, but gave bare minimum of myself. In the offering. In worship. In service.

In a way, I suppose I was like a child. Bottom lip puckered. Arms crossed. Stomping around because I didn't get my way.

I didn't want to be around anybody who'd encourage me. I kept those people at arm's length.

I felt like nobody understood what I was going through. They were all happy to live the lives they'd always known. I wasn't. I wanted more. I wanted something different.

After weeks of solitude, my joy was totally zapped. Gone. Nadda. No more.

I went to church and fulfilled my duties, but I couldn't feel God. I couldn't raise my hands to worship. I wouldn't allow praise to roll from my tongue.

Steel. Empty. Unmovable. Angry.

Anger steals your joy. Your heart cannot be joyful and angry at the same time. It's either one or the other.

Do you feel alone? Abandoned by God? Or are you the one who's pulled back and stopped communicating with God?

Bobbey Martinez, an administrative assistant, shared with me about a time she faced a similar situation. She writes:

"Several years ago, I felt God calling me towards bigger and better things, things that would have major impacts in the lives of others. But to get there, I had to give up a hobby that I dearly loved – [proofreading and/or editing] fan fiction.

The Holy Spirit was working overtime in those days and the conviction to turn away from something that was consuming me, taking me away from my family and my relationship with God was strong. But I resisted with every bit of stubbornness I had.

I made excuse after excuse; justifying to myself why I could keep doing this and still have a strong relationship with God, trying to find a way to give part of it up but not all of it, putting it aside for a little while only to pick it back up again with yet another excuse.

My family and friends knew something was wrong, but I'd pulled away and didn't want to talk about it."

Even though Bobbey felt God's conviction pulling her away from something she loved, she resisted. And through her resistance, she withdrew from the ones who cared most about her.

Bobbey goes on to say that a tire blowout on her car was the breaking point. Shaken, she called a friend, who listened as Bobbey poured out her heart. She finally came to grips that day with God's direction and released her desires to His will for her life.

The result? Bobbey's testimony says it best:

"I am now at a place where I can hear God calling me out again, and I'm getting glimpses of what I'm to be doing. The only thing I have a desire to be consumed by is my relationship with God."

GET REAL WITH GOD

When my anger reached a boiling point, I realized it wasn't just about the move.

It was about loss, heartache, heartbreak, anxiety, frustration, doubt…

Lots of old feelings and misunderstandings were being dredged up by the move. But it really wasn't about the move at all.

It was about my broken trust and faith in God.

Are you tired of being mad? Are you ready to move beyond the hurt and frustration and step into a place of peace and wholeness?

It's time to get real with God.

No matter where you are in your walk with Christ right now, I can say with complete certainty that God is there, waiting for you.

Maybe you aren't sure how to get real with God. Perhaps you've run from Him for so long now that you don't even know how to talk to Him anymore.

Sis, let me tell you...right now is the perfect time for repentance.

Right here is the perfect place for peace.

This is the moment for healing and grace.

TELL HIM WHY YOU'RE ANGRY

Life is crazy. Through death, divorce, financial problems, family issues, and addictions, we deal with frustration and bitterness every day. Before you can step out of anger and into peace, you have to get real with yourself and God.

Why are you angry at God?

This emotion must lay bare before Him. To heal, you have to expose that raw ache. Lay it at His feet.

Have you ever known someone was mad at you, but they wouldn't discuss the issue? They might have tiptoed around you, or the problem, but you could see their irritation festering under their surface of smiles and niceties.

Now imagine God in your position. He knows you're angry. He understands where that raw emotion is coming from. And He longs for you to just sit down and tell Him all about it.

You aren't punishing God through your silence. You're only hurting yourself.

Exposing this dirtiness is scary. Humbling. Freeing.

Sister, please know that when you reach the point of being undone with anger, it's in the middle of that mess God works best. He delights in comforting the broken spaces of your heart. He longs to mend those cracked places you think will never be whole again.

Did you know that Jesus, God's only Son, showed anger at times? He was as human as we. He experienced the same emotions that we do.

There isn't any better place to look for instruction on how to be angry without committing sin, than to our example—Jesus.

Even Jesus was angry at times.

If Jesus, God's only Son (chosen Son of God!) was angry, maybe we can learn from His example how to deal with our own anger.

JESUS SHOWED ANGER TOWARDS HIS DISCIPLES

On several occasions, the Bible talks about Jesus' anger displayed towards people. What I find interesting, though, is that He became angry with His disciples, too.

Mark (chapter ten) gives us an example of how this human emotion evidenced itself in Jesus. People were bringing children to Jesus for Him to bless them.

I can just imagine word spreading throughout town among parents. "Jesus is here!"

Can't you see parents scrambling to gather up their broods? "Hurry! Jesus is here," they might've said. "We must get to Jesus. We must ask His blessing over our sons and daughters."

It was no big secret who Jesus was. Curious minds were magnetized to Him, whether they believed Him to be the Messiah or not. Word of His ministry and miracles went before Him. People flocked to Jesus.

Picture all the little ones. There were probably some rambunctious boys; maybe some incredibly shy girls. Dirty fingernails. Smudged cheeks. Wonder-filled smiling eyes.

Parents probably stood behind their children. Nudged them forward, as they begged of the Master, "Please, Jesus…if You would just touch my baby's head." "Jesus, would you bless my daughter?" "Lord, bless my son…"

I can just see Jesus' face. Tender smile. Enjoying the youngsters. Delighting in their oblivious, trusting, playful souls. Knowing that He would soon give His life for these precious ones.

Then Jesus hears His disciples yelling at the moms and dads.

"Sir, step back!" Peter snaps.

"Woman, step away from the Master!" shouts John.

Andrew shoos more of the crowd away, "Get these filthy kids away from Jesus!"

And boy, was that the wrong thing for the disciples to do. The Bible says when Jesus saw what His disciples were doing, He was displeased. Mark 10:14 (NLT) says, "…he was angry with his disciples."

He gave His disciples a good tongue-lashing then gathered the children around Him. He placed His hand on their heads and blessed them.

JESUS SHOWED ANGER TOWARDS PEOPLE

> *"Jesus entered the Temple and began to drive out all the people buying and selling animals for sacrifice. He knocked over the tables of the money changers and the chairs of those selling doves."* {Matthew 21:12, NLT}

It can't be denied that Jesus had a ministry of love. His compassion shone everywhere He went. But there were moments when He'd had enough of the world. The apostle John wrote about such an incident.

Jesus went to Jerusalem for the Passover and when He arrived at the Temple, He was horrified by what He saw there. The people had turned the Temple into a common marketplace. They were selling anything and everything. Livestock grazed the area, waiting their imminent sacrifice. Shop owners haggled for deals and trades.

What a sight.

The Bible says Jesus was so mad that He made a whip to drive out the animals. Now here's where I'd like to pause for a side note. *Jesus took these people by surprise when He drove them out of the Temple.*

They were so busy making money and fulfilling their earthly desires that they didn't recognize the Master Himself had walked into the Temple. They never saw Him making a whip out of ropes.

Can you imagine with me how angry Jesus must have been? Aside from them not realizing He was even there, they'd turned the Temple into an ungodly, unholy place for their steals and deals. It must have grieved Jesus to His very core.

He was mad.

His whip crackled the air with every snap of His wrist. Sheep, cattle, and goats ran in every direction. Feathers whispered in the air as dove cages overturned to freedom.

Jesus yelled (paraphrasing), "Get this mess out of here! Don't you realize where you are? How dare you turn my Father's house into a storefront!"

JESUS WAS ANGRY AT GOD, HIS FATHER

> *"And about the ninth hour (three o'clock) Jesus cried with a loud voice, Eli, Eli, lama sabachthani?--that is, My God, My God, why have You abandoned Me [leaving Me helpless, forsaking and failing Me in My need]?"* {Matthew 27:46, AMP}

While Jesus hung on the cross, He experienced deep human emotions. From the above scripture in Matthew, you could say He was mad at God, His father.

Jesus was physically exhausted. The intense pain He endured on the cross was unspeakable and unimaginable. He was tired. Hurting. Weary. Dying.

Precious drops of blood fell to the earth beneath Him. And all the while, people mocked and made fun of Him. I can't even begin to imagine the myriad of feelings Jesus must have experienced that day.

Yet, I'm comforted by this scripture because it affirms that Jesus understands me. He experienced the same emotion—anger.

This passage affirms that when I'm mad at God, it's okay to call on Him in my anger and frustration. In fact, I *need* to tell Him when I'm angry. I need to call His name.

When I'm angry, I especially need to talk to Him and tell Him what's on my mind.

Second, it shows me that it's okay to ask those "Why me, God?" questions. "Why are You doing this to me?" "Why won't You answer my prayer?" "Why aren't you providing for my needs?" "WHY?!"

The last point I want to show you in this scripture, is probably the most important one. Listen carefully. When you're mad at God, when you don't understand His plan, when frustration has worn your mind thin…God loves you. He has a plan for your life. No amount of anger can change that.

Sis, your anger towards God does not stop Him from loving you.

It does not prevent His perfect will from coming to fruition.

The moment you're most angry at God is the perfect time to tell Him all about it. Spill your heart before Him. Then trust Him to see you through that anger and back to peace again.

HEALING RESTORATION

When I finally decided I was tired of being mad all the time, it was difficult to express myself to God. I'd been in blame mode for too long. When I'd try to pray, my prayers seemed to naturally veer off into the but-God-I-still-don't-understand-why direction.

As healing began, I turned to the Word of God for direction and wisdom.

It took many prayer sessions to refine my splintered heart and prayer life. The anger didn't die out overnight. That took some time, too. But God and I worked on it together.

In moments like these, you feel like you don't know what to say—or how to pray. Romans 8:26 (KJV) reveals to us that when we don't know what or how we should pray, "...the Spirit also helpeth our infirmities: for we know not what we should pray for as we ought:

but the Spirit itself maketh intercession for us with groanings which cannot be uttered."

I believe the best way to make that first step back to the foot of the cross is by following our Lord's example (Psalm 23). First, remind yourself of God's goodness. Remember His mercies in your life, and what He's done for you. Bring thanksgiving and repentance from your heart.

In the parable of the persistent widow (Luke 18:1-8), Jesus shares a story with his disciples about the importance of relentless prayer. Even if it's been years since you've prayed, don't give up. Keep approaching the throne. Keep bringing your offerings and sacrifices of praise before Him.

God is a just, loving, faithful, kind God.

Romans 8:31-38 (NLT) absolutely puts that myth to rest, and it specifically tells us in verse 34 that Christ Jesus gave His own life for us, "...and he is sitting in the place of honor at God's right hand, pleading for us."

But my favorite portion of this passage is in verses 38 and 39 (emphasis mine):

> *"And I am convinced that nothing can ever separate us from God's love. Neither death nor life, neither angels nor demons, neither our fears for today nor our worries about tomorrow—not even the powers of hell can separate us from God's love. No power in the sky above or in the earth below—indeed, nothing in all creation will ever be able to separate us from the love of God that is revealed in Christ Jesus our Lord."*

RECONCILE WITH GOD

Everyone has their own approach to God; every relationship is different. What I'd like to share with you is simply my approach to my relationship with God. If your walk is different, I pray something I say will spark a suggestion of how you can apply the same principle in your own special way.

I tend to view my relationship with God similar to my human relationships. Let me give you an example.

When my husband and I met, he wooed me with sweet words, kindness, and date nights. (Having a cute dimpled smile didn't hurt anything, either.)

Over the last fourteen years, our relationship has had plenty of highs and lows. We've worked through tons of issues and problems. We've experienced sadness and sorrow. We've experienced blessings and joy. Triumph and victory.

About three years into our marriage, we hit a speed bump. It nearly broke us. Our relationship strained. We barely saw each other in passing. He worked days and I worked second shift. The longer our schedule stayed this way, the wider the rift between us increased.

I was fed up. Checked out. Tired of trying.

In the middle of that mess, we turned to the wisdom of a trusted advisor. We were instructed to wake up early every morning and pray together before we started our day. I have to be honest with you. Though I complied, it was begrudgingly in the beginning. I didn't want to pray with my husband. I just wanted my space.

I wanted to be alone.

But God blessed those early morning prayer meetings. Husband and me on bended knees at the worn-out couch. Asking God to be glue and hold us together. Strengthen us to climb this mountain. Heal those wounds.

And He did. One day—one step—at a time. But it took work.

It took weeks of love notes. For-no-special-reason phone calls. Surprise visits at work, lunch in hand. It took months of *work*.

Sis, it will take the same kind of work to reconcile your relationship with God.

It might not happen overnight. It will take a continuous daily process of falling in love with Him all over again. Feasting on His word. Communicating with Him daily. Accepting His will and trusting Him to lead you. Believing in the purpose He has for your life.

It took me nearly a year to reconcile with God and allow Him to heal the anger and grief in my heart over our move to Louisiana. Those were some long, rough months.

I cried. Whined. Begged.

Then I accepted. Forgave. Repented.

He turned my weeping into joy. He turned my mourning into gladness.

Best of all, He's given me sweet peace. Now I can say with complete certainty that I know, without a doubt, I'm where God wants me to be. He is sifting and molding me into what He knows I can become in Him.

The anger you've harbored towards God may take time to scrub out of your heart. It didn't show up overnight, and it won't pack its bags and check out early, either. You'll have to work at it.

Persist at rekindling your first love with God.

GUARD YOUR SOUL & MIND

You now have an important task at hand. This might be the most crucial piece to the puzzle. Those who find themselves back in the seat of anger again usually do so because they've forgotten this specific key: Guard your soul and mind.

I'd say 99.99% of our battles begin in the mind. It's one of our most powerful weapons. It must be swept clean and polished every single day.

My husband and I recently reflected on our marriage, family, church—just life in general. I caught myself thinking those old thoughts.

My kids would be so much better off if...

I wish God would see fit to...

Then my husband made a statement that snapped me back into the reality of God's truth. He looked at me and said, "You might think I'm crazy, but I believe we are right where we're meant to be."

I wholeheartedly agree.

No, things aren't exactly the way I'd like them to be. But I've learned enough in my thirty-five years to know that when I'm in the center of God's will, my life is filled with peace. I've been on the outside, and trust me when I tell you it isn't fun.

First Peter 1:13 (NLT) explains that we should, "...think clearly and exercise self-control." Despite what some might believe, the devil can't put thoughts in your mind. It's impossible. He can plant deceptive seeds, but you make the choice to dwell on those thoughts or not.

The Word further tells us in this same chapter that we are to live holy lives. We are to follow in the footsteps of Christ. We must be obedient children of God. When we break from that submission, we invite satan to come right back and attack us again.

Peter further instructs us in verse fourteen, "Don't slip back into your old ways of living to satisfy your own desires. You didn't know any better then."

How do you guard your soul and mind? By putting on the whole armor of God (Ephesians 6:13-18, KJV).

It takes commitment.

Every single day.

Are you ready to make that commitment today? Jesus is ready. Waiting. He'll meet you there.

ABOUT THE AUTHOR

Hope Wilbanks authors the increasingly popular blog Mending Hope, where she writes to minister to the needs of Christian women.

Hope survived through nearly eighteen years of a traumatic childhood. She understands the pain of abuse and loss. She knows what shaken-faith feels like.

Today Hope writes and speaks to reach the needs of women who are dealing with their own hurts and pains. She encourages women to walk closer to God through practical, faith-building lessons.

Hope has been married for fourteen years to Robert. Together they have two amazing children. When she isn't writing or studying, Hope enjoys creating inspiring pieces of art and curling up with Peanut (her Chihuahua) and a good book.

Made in the USA
Lexington, KY
15 August 2018